Celebrate BIRTHDAYS

Birthdays are meant to be fun days, so bring on the balloons, banners, and bubbles! These two collections of party decorations and games are loaded with easy DIY projects and ideas. Create a carnival mood or get the excitement going with pinwheels and cookie pops.

LEISURE ARTS, INC. • Maumelle, Arkansas

Carnival Party

Balloon Flowers, Happy Birthday Banner & Carnival Banner instructions on pages 4-5.

Popcorn Bags instructions on page 6.

Party Hats instructions on page 8.

Popper Invitation

SHOPPING LIST

For each invitation:

- ☐ spring-loaded party popper
- ☐ assorted scrapbook papers (patterned & solid)
- ☐ double-sided tape or craft glue
- ☐ fine-point permanent pen

To make the Invitation:

1. Measure around the party popper and add 1/2"; measure the height, stopping at the twistable area of the popper. Cut a piece of patterned scrapbook paper these measurements. Cut a patterned scrapbook paper circle to fit on the popper top.
2. For the labels, determine the height of the large solid scrapbook paper piece. Print (by hand or computer) the invitation details (date, time, location, etc.) on scrapbook paper being sure the information will fit within the determined area. Print "Twist" several times in a area that is about 1/2" high and will fit around the popper (plus 1/2"). Cut the solid paper pieces. Draw the arrows on the narrow strip. Cut a 1/8" x 3" strip of solid paper.
3. Adhere the papers to each other and to the popper.

"Carnival" Pennant Banner

SHOPPING LIST

- ☐ red/white & yellow/white striped scrapbook paper or cardstock
- ☐ blue scrapbook paper or cardstock
- ☐ 2 3/4" high alphabet stickers to spell "carnival"
- ☐ 7/8" wide blue glitter ribbon (we used a 90" length)
- ☐ 9 1" diameter red tinsel pom-poms
- ☐ decorative-edge scissors
- ☐ craft glue
- ☐ tracing paper

To make the Banner:

1. Trace the pennant pattern (page 23) onto tracing paper; cut out. Use the pattern to cut 4 red/white pennants and 4 yellow/white pennants.
2. Cut 8 blue 4" diameter circles with the decorative-edge scissors. Glue a circle to each pennant.
3. Arrange the pennant on a work surface, alternating the colors and spacing them about 1" apart. Adhere the stickers to the pennants, spelling out "carnival".
4. Apply a line of glue at the top of each pennant. Placing the center of the ribbon between the "n" and the "i", adhere the ribbon to the pennants. Glue a pom-pom to the ribbon on either side of each pennant.

Balloon Flower

SHOPPING LIST

For each flower:

- ☐ $3^1/_2$" diameter cardboard circle
- ☐ 7" balloons (5 red, 1 yellow)
- ☐ craft knife
- ☐ tape

Fig. 1

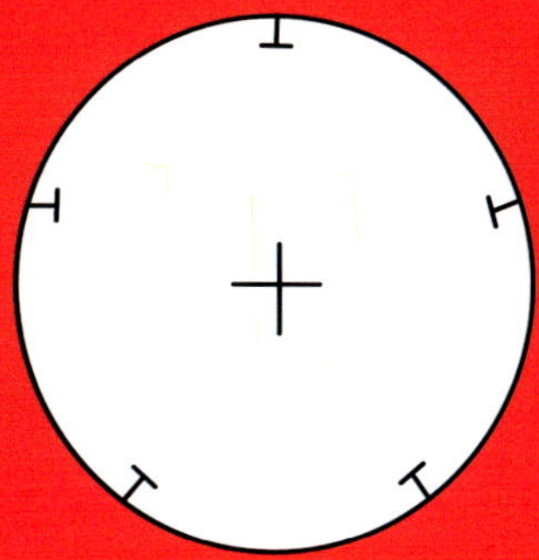

To make the Flower:

1. Referring to **Fig. 1**, use the craft knife to make slits in the cardboard circle.
2. Inflate the balloons. Pull the knot of the yellow balloon through the center slit and tape down. Pull the knots of the red balloons through the outer edge slits and tape down.

"Happy Birthday" Banner

SHOPPING LIST

- ☐ red cardstock
- ☐ red/white dotted scrapbook paper or cardstock
- ☐ blue glitter cardstock
- ☐ $^3/_4$" high alphabet stickers to spell "HAPPY BIRTHDAY"
- ☐ $^7/_8$" wide blue glitter ribbon (we used a 72" length)
- ☐ $1^3/_4$" diameter flower/starburst paper punch
- ☐ craft glue

To make the Banner:

1. Cut 13 red $3^1/_2$" diameter circles and 13 dotted 3" diameter circles. Punch 13 blue glitter flowers/starbursts.
2. Layer and glue the dotted circles on the red circles. Layer and glue the blue glitter flowers/starbursts on the dotted circles. Adhere the stickers to the circles.
3. Lay the ribbon, right side up, on a work surface. Glue the circles to the ribbon, starting at the ribbon center with the "B" and the "I" and spelling out "HAPPY BIRTHDAY".

Popcorn Bags

SHOPPING LIST

For each bag:

- ☐ white lunch bag
- ☐ red/white striped scrapbook paper
- ☐ blue scrapbook paper
- ☐ patterned yellow scrapbook paper
- ☐ craft glue
- ☐ tracing paper
- ☐ popcorn

To make the Bag:

1. Cut a 3$^{1}/_{2}$" x 5$^{1}/_{2}$" piece of striped scrapbook paper. Cut a $^{3}/_{4}$" x 5$^{1}/_{2}$" strip of blue scrapbook paper. Trace the bow and streamer patterns (page 22) onto tracing paper; cut out. Use the patterns to cut the pieces from yellow scrapbook paper. Cut a $^{1}/_{4}$" x 1$^{3}/_{8}$" strip of yellow scrapbook paper.
2. For the bow, fold each end to the center and glue. Wrap the $^{1}/_{4}$" strip around the bow and glue in place on the back. Glue the bow to the streamers.
3. Layer and glue the striped piece, the blue strip, and the yellow bow on the bag. Fill the bag with popcorn.

Photo Props

SHOPPING LIST

- ☐ Assorted cardstock (solids, patterns & glitter)
- ☐ $5^3/_4$" long craft sticks (one for each prop)
- ☐ $^1/_4$" diameter hole punch
- ☐ black fine-point permanent marker
- ☐ tracing paper
- ☐ craft glue

To make the Props:

1. Trace the patterns (pages 21 and 22) onto tracing paper; cut out. Use the patterns to cut the pieces from the desired cardstock.
2. Referring to the photo, glue the cardstock pieces together. For the big smile, use the fine-point marker to draw in the teeth lines. Glue a craft stick to the back of each prop.

Party Hats

SHOPPING LIST

For each hat:

- ☐ red/white dotted $3\frac{3}{4}$" x $2\frac{1}{2}$" paper snack bowl
- ☐ stiff felt (red or black)
- ☐ $\frac{3}{8}$" wide blue glitter ribbon
- ☐ yellow felt & 1" red tinsel pom-pom (for flower hat)
- ☐ large-eye hand sewing needle
- ☐ 20" length of black elastic cord
- ☐ tracing paper
- ☐ hot glue gun & glue sticks

To make each Hat:

1. For the hat brim, cut a red or black felt $5\frac{1}{2}$" diameter circle. For the hat top, cut red or black felt that fits the bottom of the snack bowl (which becomes the top of the hat). For the chin strap, thread the needle with the elastic cord and knot one end. Thread the needle through the larger circle about 1" from the edge; thread the needle back through the circle on the opposite side about 1" from the edge. Knot the end.
2. Centering the snack bowl on the hat brim and covering the elastic cord knots, glue the rim of the bowl to the hat brim. Glue the smaller felt circle to the hat top.
3. *For the flower hat*, trace the flower pattern (page 23) onto tracing paper; cut out. Use the pattern to cut a yellow felt flower. Glue the pom-pom to the flower center. Glue a length of blue glitter ribbon to the hat for the hat band. Cut two $4\frac{1}{2}$" lengths of blue glitter ribbon. Glue the center of the felt flower to the hat. Fold the ribbon lengths in half and glue the ends behind the flowers to create "leaves".
4. *For the bow hat,* glue a length of blue glitter ribbon to the hat for the hat band. Cut a 4" and a 1" length of blue glitter ribbon. Loop the longer length into a bow; wrap the shorter length around the bow center and glue in place. Glue the bow to the hat band.

Event Sign

SHOPPING LIST

- ☐ 11 1/2" x 8 3/4" beveled wood plaque for base
- ☐ 36" length of 3/4" square dowel
- ☐ 2 1/2" wood screw and screwdriver
- ☐ red glossy spray paint
- ☐ black foam core board
- ☐ striped & dotted scrapbook papers
- ☐ 3" high black alphabet stickers
- ☐ scrap of yellow stiff felt
- ☐ 1" red tinsel pom-pom
- ☐ tracing paper
- ☐ spray adhesive
- ☐ craft knife
- ☐ hot glue gun & glue sticks
- ☐ drill & drill bit that will make correct size hole for screw

To make the Sign:

1. Spray the wood plaque and dowel red with 2 coats of paint; allow to dry. Drill a hole in the center of the plaque and in the center of one end of the dowel. Screw the dowel to the plaque.
2. For each sign, arrange the stickers on scrapbook paper, spelling the desired words. Cut out a simple arrow shape. Use spray adhesive to adhere the scrapbook paper to the foam core board, allowing about 2" between pieces. Use the craft knife the cut arrows about 1/2" away from the scrapbook paper edges. Hot glue the signs to the dowel.
3. Trace the flower pattern (page 23) onto tracing paper; cut out. Use the pattern to cut a felt flower. Hot glue the flower to the dowel and the pom-pom to the flower.

Streamer Background

SHOPPING LIST

- ☐ 54" x 108" plastic table covers (1 each: red, yellow & white)
- ☐ stapler & staples

To make the Background:

1. Unfold each table cover. Matching the outer edges, stack all three covers. Staple one long edge together about 1" from the edge; this will be the background top. Trim 9" from one short end of the stack. Varying the colors, cut 33 1" x 9" strips from the trimmed away edges to use as ties; set aside.
2. Beginning at one short side, cutting through all layers, and stopping about 8" from the top, cut 3" wide streamers across the table cover stack.
3. Braid each set of streamers together for about 3". Secure the braid by tying a 9" strip around the streamers; trim the tie ends as desired.

Cans

Ramp up the festivites with these colorful upcycled containers! Just cover clean soup or vegetable cans with scrapbook paper and you've got an instant ball toss game.

Ring Toss Game

SHOPPING LIST

- ☐ 6 colored-glass soda bottles
- ☐ play sand
- ☐ 3 4" diameter steel rings
- ☐ 2 1/2 yards paracord for each ring (we used red & yellow)
- ☐ solid & patterned cardstock
- ☐ decorative-edge scissors
- ☐ craft glue
- ☐ double-sided tape

To make the Game:

1. To make the rings, tie a paracord length to a ring, leaving about a 1" tail. Work half-hitch knots ***(Fig. 1)*** around the entire ring, covering the beginning tail and completely covering the ring. Tuck the cord end under a knot and trim the excess. Apply a generous amount of craft glue to the cut end and surrounding area. Set aside and allow the glue to dry.

Fig. 1

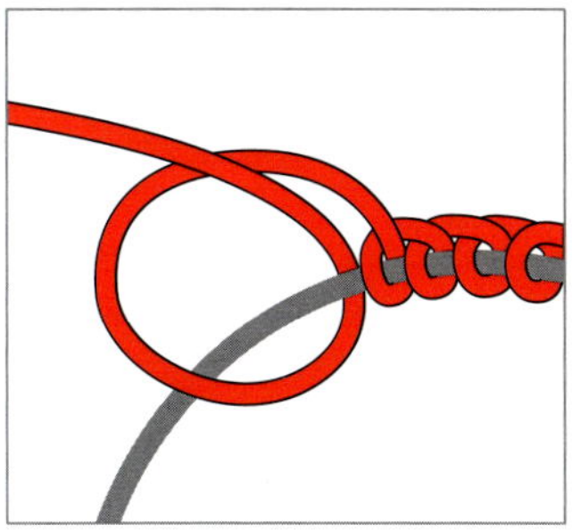

2. To decorate the bottles with scoring tags, cut six 3 1/2" diameter solid cardstock circles with the decorative-edge scissors. Cut six 3" diameter contrasting solid color cardstock circles. Print (by hand or computer) 2 5/8" high numbers (0, 1, 3, 5) to use as patterns. Use these number patterns to cut two 3's, two 5's, two 1's, and two 0's from patterned cardstock. Layer and glue the circles and numbers to create the scoring tags. Adhere the tags to the bottles with double-sided tape.

Treats & Sweets Party

Giant Swirls
instructions on page 20.

Balloon "Ice Cream Cones"

SHOPPING LIST

For each cone:

- ☐ 9" balloon
- ☐ tissue paper to match balloon color
- ☐ 12" x 12" kraft paper cardstock
- ☐ 20" white balloon stick
- ☐ brown permanent marker
- ☐ tracing paper
- ☐ double-sided tape
- ☐ colored soda bottle with sand

To make the Cone:

1. Trace the cone pattern (page 24) onto tracing paper; cut out. Use the pattern to cut the cone from cardstock. Referring to the pattern, use the brown marker to draw a 3/4" diagonal grid on the cardstock. Roll the cardstock into a cone and secure with double-sided tape.
2. Cut 3" squares of tissue paper (we cut 16 squares). Adhere a strip of double-sided tape along the inside top edge of the cardstock cone. Pleat and adhere the tissue paper squares to the tape.
3. Inflate the balloon and attach it to the balloon stick. Insert the balloon stick into the cone. Use bits of double-sided tape to hold the cone in place.
4. Place the cones in the sand-filled soda bottle.

Pinwheel Treat Bottle

SHOPPING LIST

For each bottle:

- ☐ double-sided cardstock
- ☐ 3/8" diameter colored brad
- ☐ kraft paper drinking straw
- ☐ mini milk bottle
- ☐ candy to fill bottle
- ☐ 1/8" diameter hole punch
- ☐ tracing paper
- ☐ hot glue gun and glue sticks

To make the Bottle:

1. Trace the pattern (page 22) onto tracing paper; cut out. Use the pattern to cut the pinwheel from cardstock; cut in toward the center as indicated on the pattern. Punch holes as indicated on the pattern
2. Fold each point with a hole to the center, aligning the holes with the center hole and forming the pinwheel. Insert the brad through the holes and open the prongs on the back. Hot glue the pinwheel to the straw.
3. Fill the bottle with candy and insert the straw.

Party Banner

SHOPPING LIST

- ☐ assorted cardstock
- ☐ 2" high alphabet stickers to spell "PARTY"
- ☐ paper twine (we used a 72" length)
- ☐ ten $1^3/_4$" long clothespins
- ☐ tracing paper
- ☐ craft glue

To make the Banner:

1. Trace the pennant pattern (page 23) onto tracing paper; cut out. Use the pattern to cut 5 pennants from the assorted cardstock. Cut five 3" diameter circles from cardstock.
2. Layer and glue the circles on the pennants. Adhere the stickers to the circles.
3. Clip the pennants to the twine, spelling out "PARTY".

Cookie Pops

SHOPPING LIST

For each pop:

- ☐ mega-stuffed cream-filled sandwich cookie
- ☐ ready-to-use frosting
- ☐ candy sprinkles
- ☐ lollipop stick
- ☐ 3" x 4" treat bag
- ☐ 9" length of $^5/_8$" wide ribbon

To make the Cookie Pop:

1. Carefully insert the lollipop stick into the cream filling of the cookie. Spread frosting on the cookie and add sprinkles. Allow the frosting to harden.
2. Place the pop in the treat bag. Tie the ribbon bow around the bag and the lollipop stick.

Lemonade Bottles

SHOPPING LIST

For each bottle:

- ☐ mini milk bottle
- ☐ 9" x 1" strip of scrapbook paper
- ☐ kraft paper tag
- ☐ "Happy Birthday" stamp
- ☐ black permanent ink pad
- ☐ bakers twine (2 colors)
- ☐ double-sided tape
- ☐ white permanent marker
- ☐ kraft paper straw
- ☐ lemonade

To make the Bottle:

1. Stamp "Happy Birthday" on the scrapbook paper strip. Wrap the strip around the bottle near the bottom and secure with double-sided tape.
2. Write the guest's name on the tag. Cut a 24" length of each color of twine. Wrap the twine lengths around the neck of the bottle 3 times, slip the tag on the twine, and tie a bow.
3. Fill the bottle with lemonade and insert the straw.

Favor Bag

SHOPPING LIST

For each bag:

- ☐ brown lunch bag
- ☐ striped scrapbook paper
- ☐ contrasting color scrapbook paper
- ☐ kraft paper tag
- ☐ bakers twine
- ☐ $^{1}/_{4}$" diameter hole punch
- ☐ permanent marker
- ☐ craft glue
- ☐ favors to go in bag

To make the Bag:

1. Cut a $5^{1}/_{2}$" x 6" piece of the striped scrapbook paper. Cut a $5^{1}/_{2}$" x $1^{1}/_{4}$" strip of contrasting scrapbook paper. Layer and glue the contrasting strip on the striped paper.
2. Fill the bag with favors and fold the bag top toward the front. Glue the paper on the bag; punch two holes about 1" apart at the top center of the bag, punching through all layers of the bag and paper.
3. Cut two 18" lengths of bakers twine. Write the guest's name on the tag. Thread the twine through the holes, slip the tag on the twine, and tie a bow to keep the bag closed.

Bubble Station

Bubbles bring out the kid in everyone! Pick up a Bubble Party Kit and a bottle of Bubble "juice"; then, decorate the dispenser bottle and individual cups with colorful scrapbook paper and let the party begin!

Giant Swirls

SHOPPING LIST

For each swirl:

- ☐ 12" x 12" sheet of cardstock
- ☐ 1/8" diameter hole punch
- ☐ string to hang the swirl

To make the Swirl:

1. Draw an 11 1/2" circle on the cardstock; cut out.
2. Starting at an edge and referring to **Fig. 1**, cut the circle into a spiral.

Fig. 1

3. Punch a hole at the center of the swirl. Thread the string through the hole to hang the swirl.

Patterns

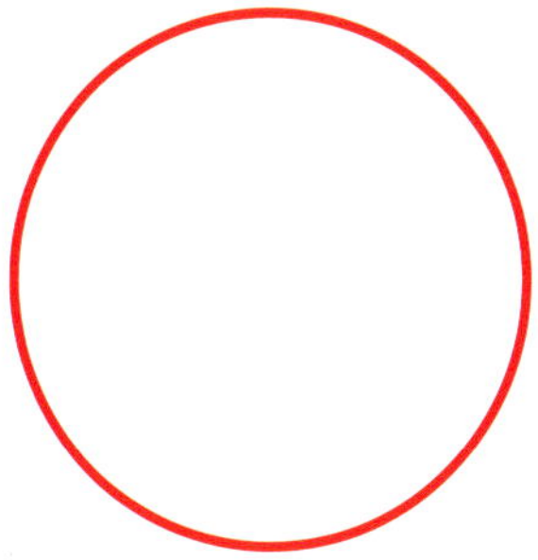

Photo Props

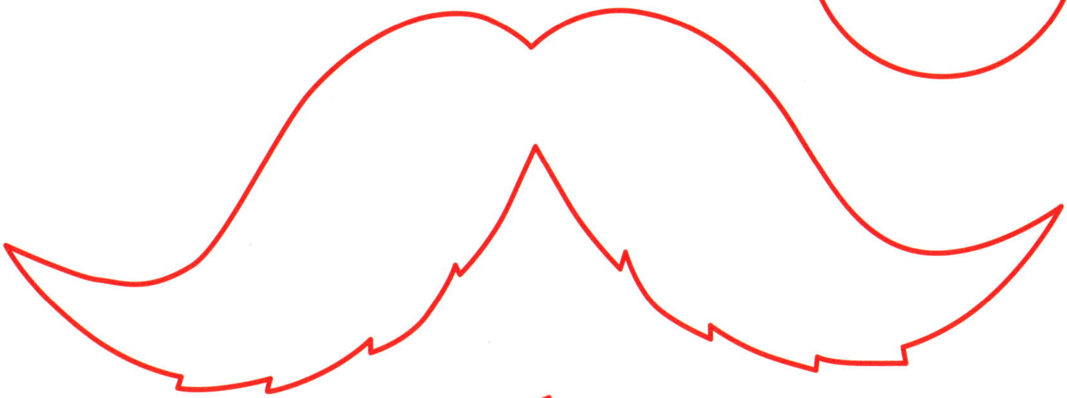

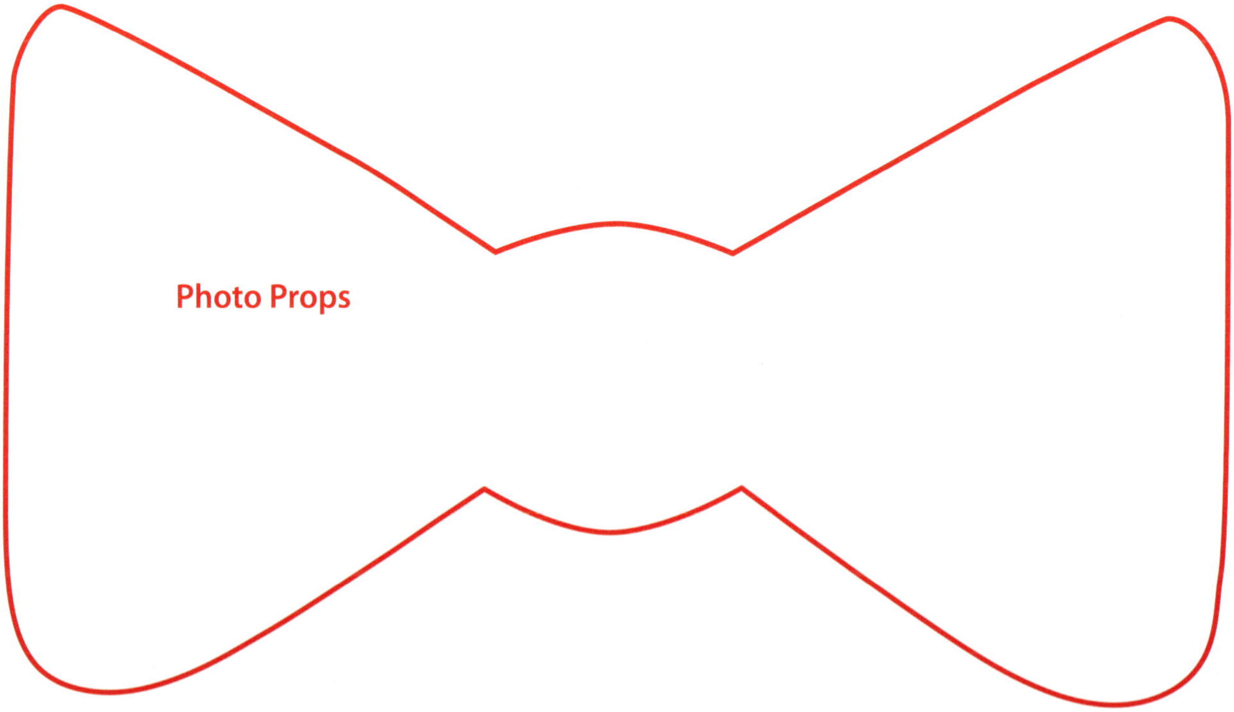

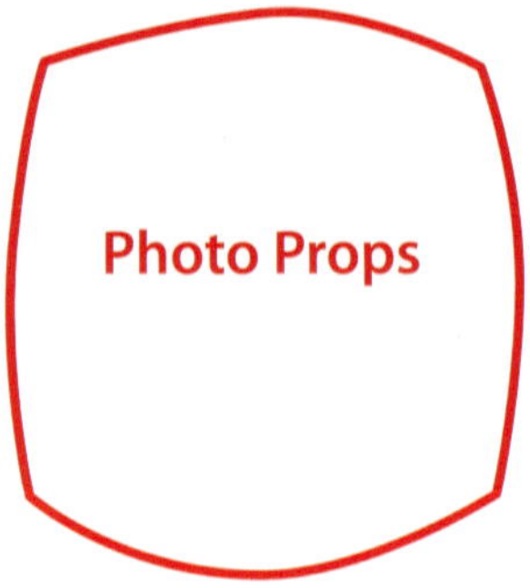

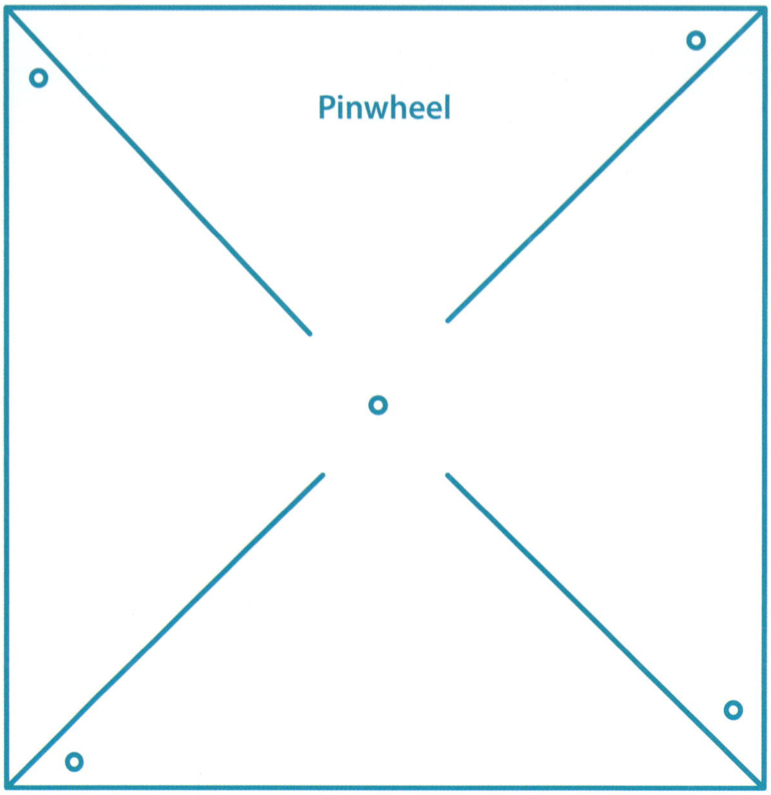

Popcorn
Bag Streamers

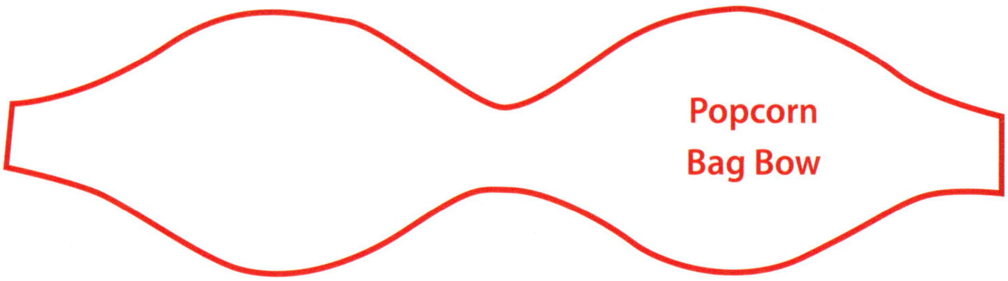

"Carnival" Pennant Banner
"Party" Banner
Party Hat/
Event Sign
Flower

Balloon "Ice Cream Cones"

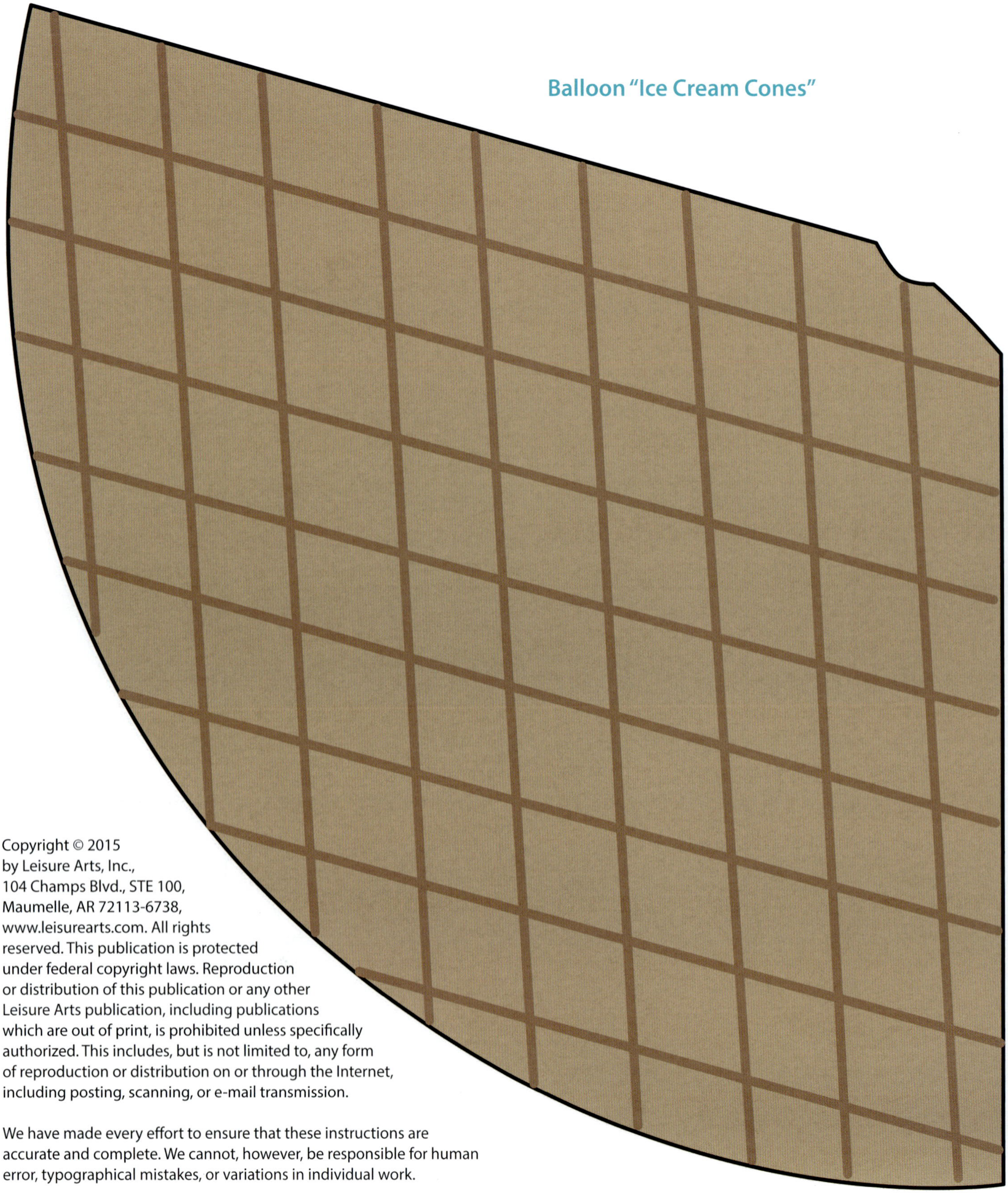

Production Team: Product Development Director: Anna L. Andrews; Designer – Kelly Reider; Contributing Designer – Becky Werle; Technical Writer – Mary Sullivan Hutcheson; Technical Associate – Frances Huddleston; Editorial Writer – Susan Frantz Wiles; Senior Graphic Artist – Lora Puls; Photostylist – Lori Wenger; Photographer – Jason Masters.